BALLOON PUBLISHING

COLOR TEST PAGE

It's just
a bad day,
Not
a bad life

It is the
season
to
SPARKLE

Never,
NEVER,
never
Give Up!

LIVE
LAUGH
LOVE

Beautiful
Minds
Inspire
Others

Better
an
Oops
than a
What if

GIVE
thanks
WITH A
grateful
HEART

The most
important
things *in*
life
aren't
things

DON'T be THE SAME
BE BETTER

YOU
MELT
MY
HEART

Eat
Sleep
Love
Repeat

Live
LIFE
to the
FULL

WORK
HARD
STAY
HUMBLE

THERE
are NO
REGRETS
in life,
JUST
LESSONS

LIFE
is
WHAT
YOU
MAKE

Work Hard Stay Humble

Today
is
always
the
Best
DAY

SOMETIMES
LATER
BECOMES
NEVER
DO IT
NOW

Love
is
in the
AIR

our
story
BEGINS
here

DON'T
STOP
believing

Wishes
come
TRUE

What Does The Fox Say

Have
courage
and be
kind

THERE'S
always
SOMETHING
TO BE
thankful
FOR

No
Sweet
Without
Sweat

Keep
Life
SIMPLE

you can do
EVERYTHING

Made in the USA
Monee, IL
19 June 2020

33865885R00037